The Next Frontier

IEEE

IEEE⊕computer society

⊕CSPress

Press Operating Committee

Chair

James W. Cortada
IBM Institute for Business Value

Board Members

Mark J. Christensen, Independent Consultant

Richard E. (Dick) Fairley, Founder and Principal Associate, Software Engineering Management Associates (SEMA)

Cecilia Metra, Associate Professor of Electronics, University of Bologna

Linda Shafer, former Director, Software Quality Institute, The University of Texas at Austin

Evan Butterfield, Director of Products and Services

Kate Guillemette, Product Development Editor, CS Press

The Next Frontier

Managing Data Confidentiality
and Integrity in the Cloud

by Francisco Rocha, Salvador Abreu, and Miguel Correia

Page design by Monette Velasco.

ISBN-10: 0-7695-4978-0
ISBN-13: 978-0-7695-4978-1

Contents

Chapter 1:
Introduction

Many companies have embraced the benefits of cloud computing because of its pay-per-use cost model and the elasticity of resources that it provides. But from a data confidentiality and integrity viewpoint, moving a company's IT systems to a *public cloud* poses some challenges. System protection is often based on perimeter security, but in the cloud, the company's systems run on the cloud provider's hardware and coexist with software from both the provider and other cloud service consumers. Simply put, the cloud blurs the formerly clear separation between the trusted inside and the untrusted outside.

Although researchers have identified numerous security threats to the cloud,[1] malicious insiders still represent a significant concern. This security threat takes

---

1   Cloud Security Alliance, *Top Threats to Cloud Computing*, vol. 1, Mar. 2010; https://cloudsecurityalliance.org/topthreats/csathreats.v1.0.pdf.

on new dimensions in this environment, as cloud operators and system administrators are unseen, unknown, and not onsite. Confidential data such as passwords, cryptographic keys, or files are just a few commands away from access by a malicious or incompetent system administrator.

The existence of a malicious insider in a cloud provider may seem improbable, but reality shows that it can happen. In 2010 an engineer was fired from Google for violating the privacy of some of their users.[2] In 2009, an ex-employee of CyberLynk, a cloud storage provider, logged into the company's systems and deleted a large amount of data—a season of a TV series—leading to a lawsuit.[3] Moreover, a recent report about the CERT's insider threat database found more than 550 insider attacks, including cases of sabotage, fraud, and intellectual property theft.[4] This report, however, was not in the context of cloud computing.

Cloud providers are well aware of these concerns, as demonstrated in a recent roundtable including senior staff representing some of the sector's major companies.[5] One participant stated that his company has "very strict procedures in place for when our employees are allowed to access the machines the customer data resides on. We keep track of every action they take on those machines, and we log all that information for later audits so that we can ensure that all employees are behaving consistently with our privacy policy." Another participant added, "We have zero tolerance for insiders abusing that trust."

Although these policies are important—even essential—they fall short of solving the problem. Preventing physical access is not effective against remote attacks, and monitoring or auditing only detects an attack after it happens, which is usually too late. Interestingly, a participant in that same roundtable replied to a question about security and trust in the cloud that "there are some things that will never go into [the cloud], for example, our SAP back end."

So how can an organization store confidential and private data in the cloud in a way that prevents its disclosure or modification by malicious insiders in the cloud? How can a cloud service provider assure its users that their data is safe

2   A. Chen, "GCreep: Google Engineer Stalked Teens, Spied on Chats (Updated)," *Gawker*, 14 Sep. 2010; http://gawker.com/5637234/.

3   P. Nemani, "Hacker Deleted Entire Season, TV Station Says," *Courthouse News Service*, 31 Mar. 2011; www.courthousenews.com/2011/03/31/35406.htm.

4   M. Hanley et al., "An Analysis of Technical Observations in Insider Theft of Intellectual Property Cases," tech. report CMU/SEI-2011-TN-006, Software Eng. Inst., Carnegie Mellon Univ., 2011.

5   E. Grosse et al., "Cloud Computing Roundtable," *IEEE Security and Privacy*, Nov./Dec. 2010, pp. 17–23.

from malicious insiders? To the best of our knowledge, no single current technical approach solves this problem entirely. Instead, partial solutions include providing isolated environments,[6] some via trusted computing and the trusted platform module (TPM),[7] or exploiting cloud diversity and replication for data storage.[8]

This text presents a solution to this problem in the context of clouds that provide the *infrastructure as a service* (IaaS) model, in the sense of clouds where consumers can run virtual machines. It may also serve as a basis for implementing other cloud models, such as platform as a service (PaaS), but we do not consider those other models here.

The proposed scheme can be implemented by cloud providers with two related goals:

- to protect consumers' data from malicious insiders;
- to assure consumers that their data is protected from such adversaries.

The solution explores the notion of *trusted computing* and is based on the TPM. We introduce the architecture and main mechanisms and discuss the open challenges of the solution.

This text is complementary—it is not a substitute—to several guidelines and reports on cloud security that have been published by organizations including the National Institute of Standards and Technology (NIST),[9] the European

6   D.G. Murray, G. Milos, and S. Hand, "Improving Xen Security through Disaggregation," *Proc. 4th ACM SIGPLAN/SIGOPS Int'l Conf. Virtual Execution Environments* (VEE 08), ACM, 2008, pp. 151–160; and U. Steinberg and B. Kauer, "NOVA: A Microhypervisor-Based Secure Virtualization Architecture," *Proc. 5th European Conf. Computer Systems* (EuroSys 10), ACM, 2010, pp. 209–222.

7   J.M. McCune et al., "TrustVisor: Efficient TCB Reduction and Attestation," *Proc. IEEE Symp. Security and Privacy* (SSP 10), IEEE CS, 2010, pp.143–158; N. Santos et al., "Policy-Sealed Data: A New Abstraction for Building Trusted Cloud Services," *Proc. 21st USENIX Security Symp.*, USENIX, Aug. 2012, p. 10; and F. Zhang et al., "CloudVisor: Retrofitting Protection of Virtual Machines in Multi-tenant Cloud with Nested Virtualization," *Proc. 23rd ACM Symp. Operating Systems Principles* (SOSP 11), ACM, Oct. 2011, pp. 203–216.

8   A. Bessani et al., "DepSky: Dependable and Secure Storage in a Cloud-of-Clouds," *Proc. European Conf. Computer Systems* (EuroSys 11), ACM, 2011, pp. 31–46; and K.D. Bowers, A. Juels, and A. Oprea, "HAIL: a High-Availability and Integrity Layer for Cloud Storage," *Proc. 16th ACM Conf. Computer and Communications Security* (CCS 09), ACM, 2009, pp. 187–198.

9   W. Jansen and T. Grance, *Guidelines on Security and Privacy in Public Cloud Computing*, special publication 800-144, Nat'l Inst. Standards and Technology, Dec. 2011.

Network and Information Security Agency (ENISA),[10] and the Cloud Security Alliance.[11] These documents provide extremely important advice on cloud computing security but, although they recognize the importance of the malicious insider threat, they do not provide solutions to this problem. Nevertheless, they mention many important security mechanisms that we do not cover.

This document is organized as follows:

- Chapter 2 presents basic concepts of cloud computing, including models and the cloud virtualized infrastructure;
- Chapter 3 introduces trusted computing concepts and mechanisms;
- Chapter 4 presents the two protection schemes proposed: basic and enhanced;
- Chapter 5 discusses related work and alternative approaches;
- Chapter 6 concludes the discussion.

---

10 D. Catteddu and G. Hogben, eds., *Cloud Computing: Benefits, Risks and Recommendations for Information Security*, European Network and Information Security Agency, 2009.
11 G. Brunette and R. Mogull, eds., *Security Guidance for Critical Areas of Focus in Cloud Computing V2.1*, Cloud Security Alliance, 2009.

Chapter 2:
Cloud Computing

T his chapter provides background on cloud computing. It starts by introducing the cloud computing models, providing insight on how the cloud is used. Then it explains the architecture of a cloud computing environment and gives an example of cloud management software, Eucalyptus. This background is important in understanding the malicious insider problem in the cloud and how it can be dealt with.

2.1 Cloud Computing Models

The NIST has earned an important role in cloud computing by publishing a landmark document defining its main concepts.[1] Although very short, this doc-

---

1   P. Mell and T. Grance, *The NIST Definition of Cloud Computing (Draft)*, special publication 800-145 (draft), Nat'l Inst. Standards and Technology, Jan. 2011.

ument established a set of terms that have become well accepted. We follow its nomenclature throughout the text.

Deployment Models

NIST defined four *deployment models* for the cloud: private cloud, community cloud, public cloud, and hybrid cloud.

A *private cloud* is dedicated to service the organization that owns it. This type of infrastructure is usually deployed and managed within the organization's premises, but deployment and management can as well be outsourced to a third party.

The purpose of a *community cloud* is to provide an infrastructure to be shared among institutions with common interests (e.g., mission or security requirements). Like a private cloud, it can be deployed and managed by the owner organizations or by a third party.

The *public cloud* model involves a cloud provider selling cloud services to consumer organizations. These services are deployed and managed in the provider's infrastructure. The public cloud is the quintessential cloud deployment model.

A *hybrid cloud* is simply a combination of two or more clouds from any of the previous models.

Service Models

The NIST defined three cloud *service models*: infrastructure as a service (IaaS), platform as a service (PaaS), and software as a service (SaaS). We present them considering the case of a public cloud, although the service models are orthogonal to the deployment models.

Starting with the latter, in the *software as a service* (SaaS) model the cloud provider offers consumers applications running on the cloud infrastructure, typically web applications. Obvious examples are Google Docs (docs.google.com), Microsoft Office 365 (www.office365.com), and Yahoo! Mail (mail.yahoo.com). The consumer can access services through thin clients running on multiple devices, usually a web browser or a mobile device app. The level of control is the lowest of all models: the consumer has no control over the infrastructure or the software executed; he or she can only configure some application preferences.

Platform as a service (PaaS) grants more control to the consumer. In this model the cloud provides an application development and execution platform. Consumers develop their own applications in the cloud platform using a set of components it provides. Example commercial PaaS offerings include Salesforce's Force.com (www.salesfore.com/platform), Microsoft Windows Azure (www.windowsazure.com), and Google AppEngine (appengine.google.com). There

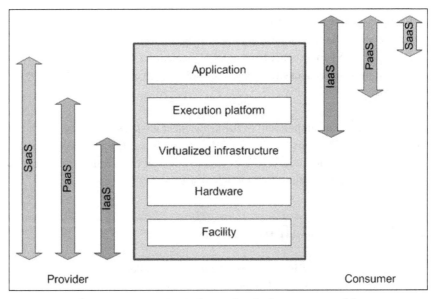

Figure 1. Provider vs. consumer scope and control in the three service models.

is also PaaS platform software available, including VMware's Cloud Foundry (www.cloudfoundry.com), Salesforce's Heroku (www.heroku.com), and Red Hat's Open Shift (openshift.redhat.com).

The third service model, *infrastructure as a service* (IaaS), is the one that provides the highest level of control to the consumer. An IaaS offering provides basic computing resources: processing, storage, and network. The most common cases offer the ability to run full virtual machines, as in Amazon EC2 (aws.amazon.com/ec2), or data storage, as in Amazon S3 (aws.amazon.com/s3). Offerings that allow consumers to run virtual machines give them much control, as it is the consumers who select and install their own operating systems and application software. However, the underlying cloud infrastructure is still administered by the cloud provider.

Figure 1[2] abstracts cloud hardware and software in terms of a stack and shows the scope and control of the cloud provider (left) and consumer (right) for each service model.

This text is mostly concerned with clouds that follow the *IaaS service model* and, specifically, that execute *virtual machines* on behalf of their users. The reasons for considering IaaS instead of PaaS or SaaS are mainly two:

---

2   Jansen and Grance, 2011.

- it is the simplest service model and the one that gives more control to the consumer, so it is the easiest to analyze and protect from malicious behavior;
- PaaS and SaaS can be considered as additional layers on top of an IaaS service, so IaaS security is necessary even in clouds that provide these other service models.

Our approach is independent of the *deployment model*, so it can be any of the four which were previously discussed. However, the administration of the machines that access the cloud should be independent of the administration of the cloud; therefore, the public cloud model is the most obvious use case.

2.2 Virtualized Infrastructure

The main enabler of IaaS is *native virtualization*, also called type I virtualization.[3] This technology first appeared in the late 1960s in IBM mainframes such as System/360. It reappeared in the late 1990s with VMware.

In native virtualization, the hardware—typically a server—runs a layer of software called a *hypervisor* or *virtual machine monitor* that supports the execution of several *virtual machines* (VMs), each with its own operating system and software instances (see Figure 2). The hypervisor essentially provides each VM with an interface that is almost indistinguishable from the hardware as well as isolation from other VMs.

Currently there are several virtualization products available. Cloud providers are using open hypervisors such as Xen (xen.org) or Linux KVM (www.linux-kvm.org), or the commercial products by VMware (www.vmware.com/products) and others. For almost a decade, hypervisors were simply a software layer, but their efficiency today relies on hardware support from mainstream processors, namely on AMD's AMD-V technology and Intel's VT-x.

Infrastructure as a Service

Public IaaS cloud offerings such as Amazon EC2 and Rackspace Cloud Servers (www.rackspace.com/cloud/public/servers), and cloud software like OpenNeb-

---

3   M. Rosenblum and T. Garfinkel, "Virtual Machine Monitors: Current Technology and Future Trends," *Computer*, vol. 38, no. 5, May 2005, pp. 39–47.

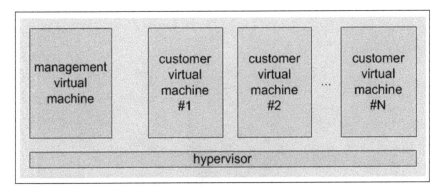

Figure 2. Software architecture of a VM server in an IaaS cloud.

ula (opennebula.org) and Eucalyptus (www.eucalyptus.com), essentially provide consumers with the ability to run their own VMs in VM servers (see Figure 2). These VMs are created from images that contain the operating system and other software (e.g., a LAMP stack or an application server such as JBoss or GlassFish). Commercial offerings normally provide some ready-to-use images, but security-wise it is advisable for consumers to create their own images with a hardened operating system and a well-configured software stack. In fact, a study has concluded that a provider's ready-to-use images contain many vulnerabilities.[4]

An IaaS cloud comprises different components with distinct functions. Figure 3 provides a very abstract view of such an infrastructure, found in Amazon EC2, OpenNebula, and Eucalyptus. The cloud is accessed by consumers and other users, e.g., those who use consumers' web applications that run in the cloud. They access the cloud through the internet (top of the figure), typically through an *access frontend*.

To launch a VM, a consumer accesses the *administration frontend* and requests this operation. This access can be obtained manually through a web interface or a command line interface, or programmatically through web services or a REST API. This frontend communicates with the *VM controller* (left) that accesses one or more management VMs in VM servers (bottom). The management VM can be, for instance, Dom0 in Xen running a daemon that processes management commands. The images are stored in the *storage* components (right).

4   S. Bugiel et al., "AmazonIA: When Elasticity Snaps Back," *Proc. 18th ACM Conf. Computer and Communications Security* (CCS 11), ACM, Oct. 2011, pp. 389–400.

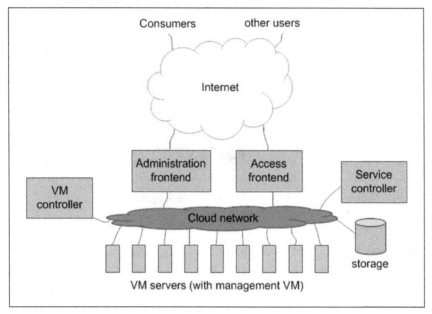

Figure 3. Simplified architecture of a public IaaS cloud.

Cloud offerings provide more services than simply instantiating VMs: load balancing, monitoring services, storage, databases, a MapReduce engine, etc. For instance, in July 2012, Amazon AWS listed around 24 of these services in its portal. In Figure 3, we abstract the components that manage these services in a box called *service controller*.

It is important to notice that the boxes in the picture are only abstractions that can be implemented by many physical devices. For instance, the cloud network is usually a complex, hierarchical subsystem,[5] the VM controller is also typically hierarchical (e.g., with one instance per cluster), and the access frontend typically includes many subcomponents, such as reverse proxies, firewalls, etc.

The figure also conveys the simplistic notion that the cloud infrastructure exists at a single location, but in reality the main cloud vendors have several datacenters scattered worldwide.

5   D. Abts and B. Felderman, "A Guided Tour of Data-Center Networking," *Communications of the ACM*, vol. 55, no. 6, June 2012, pp. 44–51.

An Example—Eucalyptus

Let us make these abstractions more concrete with the specific case of Eucalyptus (www.eucalyptus.com). This platform defines five main high-level components. These components are implemented as stand-alone services, each with its own web interface. The five components are designated: cloud controller, cluster controller, node controller, walrus, and storage controller.

The *cloud controller* (CLC) is the entry-point into the architecture, so it is equivalent to the administration frontend of Figure 3. It is responsible for exposing and managing the existing virtualized resources (processing, storage, and network). It exposes the resources through an API compatible with Amazon EC2's or a web-based consumer interface. The control or management process involves gathering information about resource availability, making high-level scheduling decisions, and working with the cluster controller to implement VM scheduling (i.e., to decide what VM runs where).

In Eucalyptus the VM servers are called *nodes* and are organized in *clusters*. A cluster is managed by a *cluster controller* (CC) that is logically located between the CLC and the nodes that form the cluster. The CC keeps information regarding VMs executing in the cluster's nodes and schedules VM operations for those nodes. The SLAs provided by the CLC are locally enforced through the CCs.

The nodes run *node controllers* (NCs) that are equivalent to our management VM. An NC manages the lifecycle of a VM, including its execution, migration, monitoring, and termination. It also fetches and cleans local copies of instance images. Each NC includes an NC agent that is responsible for querying and controlling the system software (NC and hypervisor) on behalf of the CC.

The *walrus* provides bucket-based storage, so it is part of the service controller and storage components of Figure 3. In essence, it allows consumers to store persistent data and exports an interface compatible with that of the Amazon S3 service. Similarly to S3, the walrus can be accessed from inside and outside of the cloud.

Storage capabilities reside also with the *storage controller* (SC) that is again equivalent to part of our service controller and storage. It is capable of interfacing with multiple storage systems (e.g., NFS and iSCSI), and it provides functionality similar to Amazon's Elastic Block Storage (EBS). Storage provided through the SC cannot be shared among VMs and has to be accessed from within the cloud.

Chapter 3:
Trusted Computing

To the best of our knowledge, the term *trusted computing* first appeared in the early 2000s to designate the work of what later became the Trusted Computing Group or TCG (www.trustedcomputinggroup.org). The initial idea was to improve computer security by exploiting the mechanisms of an inexpensive trustworthy chip. Hardware-based security is far from new, but the TCG made an important contribution by creating the specification for a standard hardware component, the Trusted Platform Module.[1] The specification is currently on version 1.2 and dates back to March 2011. This specification provides a TPM manufacturer with the architectural and functional details required to produce a TPM chip.

---

1   Trusted Computing Group, *TPM Main Specification*, version 1.2, revision 103, 2007; www.trustedcomputinggroup.org/resources/tpm_main_specification; and D. Grawrock, *Dynamics of a Trusted Platform: A Building Block Approach*, Intel Press, 2009.

The term trusted computing has evolved, and today it is used also to denote a set of security mechanisms included in AMD and Intel CPUs, in disks, and in mobile devices. Furthermore, some researchers have started to use the term *trustworthy computing*, which makes sense in that this technology aims to provide the grounds for systems to be trustworthy (a characteristic of the system), not only trusted (something assumed by users or other systems). However, here we use the older and more widely used term, trusted computing.

In this chapter we briefly describe the basic components of a TPM and discuss some of the security functionalities we can obtain through the use of those same components.

3.1 Trusted Platform Module

The TPM chip is currently found on the motherboard of many commercial PCs (its presence can be checked in the BIOS settings). It is an opt-in device, in the sense that the user can opt to use it or not and has to perform specific actions to turn it on. It is built to be tamperproof, providing a set of functions that the software in the PC can call with the assistance of a device driver and a library for the programming language used.

The TPM specification stipulates that it must be connected to the low pin count (LPC) bus of the PC. Therefore, the TPM is a slave device that must be called by the CPU, like any other device connected to the LPC bus. The TPM cannot interrupt the CPU or change the PC execution flow.

The TPM receives commands from the CPU and returns responses. For each command it returns a response, following a pattern similar to a remote procedure call (RPC). At low level these commands and responses can be considered to be packets with four fields: type of packet (command or response); length of packet (in bytes); command number or return code (respectively for command and response); and command data or return data (again for command/response). The TPM verifies that the received commands follow this format and are valid (e.g., command numbers correspond to valid commands).

The TPM has an execution engine that is the equivalent of the CPU in a computer. When a command is received, it calls the validation function and, if the command is valid, it calls the code that runs the command. This code can perform further validation actions (e.g., verify needed authorization), executes the requested command, and prepares the response.

Functional Units and Memory

From the viewpoint of the programmer, the TPM mostly contains functional units and memory. Table 1 presents the main components of TPM 1.1 (there are a few more in TPM 1.2).

Table 1. Trusted Platform Module 1.1 Main Components.	
Component class	**Function provided/data stored**
Functional units	Random numbers Cryptographic hashes Message authentication codes (HMAC) RSA key-pair generation RSA encryption and decryption
Nonvolatile memory	Endorsement key Storage root key Owner authorization secret key
Volatile memory	RSA key pairs Platform configuration registers Key handles Authorization session handles

The TPM's *functional units* are related to cryptography, including random number generation, key generation, hash functions, and RSA encryption (see Table 1). The TPM contains a random number generator that uses sources of entropy internal to the TPM. This random number generator is used by the RSA engine to obtain randomness in the process of RSA key generation. RSA keys are used by the TPM for encryption and signatures. The TPM specification mandates the implementation of the SHA-1 cryptographic hash algorithm that is used for several purposes (e.g., for digital signatures).

Cryptographic hash functions such as SHA-1 are *collision-resistant*, meaning that it is computationally infeasible to find a different input that provides the same output/hash. Therefore, if a certain code module has a hash h1, it is impossible to substitute a different code with the same hash h1. This property is important for measuring program code. The authors of the specification are aware of the potential weakness of SHA-1 and mention that future specifications are likely to include additional hash algorithms.

The *nonvolatile memory* stores two important public/private key pairs whose private portions never leave the TPM—the *endorsement key* (EK) and the storage root key—as well as a secret called the owner authorization secret key. The EK uniquely identifies a TPM, whereas the storage root key is used to encrypt keys to be stored outside the TPM. The content of the nonvolatile memory is persistent in the sense that it remains untouched even if the PC where the TPM resides is rebooted.

The TPM also has *volatile memory*. This area stores the items listed on Table 1. As is the case with the nonvolatile memory, external entities cannot access data stored there directly, only through certain commands. The volatile memory stores keys and handles used for different purposes. From our point of view, the most important items of the volatile memory are *platform configuration registers* (PCRs); there are at least 24, and they are at least 20 bytes long.

The PCRs are used to store *measurements*. A measurement is a cryptographic hash of executable code loaded in a memory zone. A PCR can be read—an operation called *quote* in TCG lingo. More importantly, a PCR *cannot* be directly written into; it can only be *extended*. The extend operation consists in performing an SHA-1 (function H) of the current PCR value concatenated with the new value (v): $PCR_i \leftarrow H(PCR_i \mid\mid v)$. Some interesting properties are gained from using the extend operation instead of a write/store operation. The most important in our case is that it is not possible to insert an arbitrary value in a PCR after it is first written. Two more interesting properties are that the TPM can use a single PCR to keep track of an unlimited number of measurements and that an entity cannot pretend to have extended the PCRs in a different order than the one it did. This is due to the ordering property of SHA-1 that states that $H(H(A) \mid\mid B) \neq H(H(B) \mid\mid A)$. The measurements kept by PCRs are typically used to attest to a challenging party that the PC has a certain software configuration, as we discuss in the next section.

3.2 Establishing Trust

The TPM building blocks we just described support several mechanisms that can be used to make current systems more secure. Next, we present in more detail those that are relevant to the problem discussed in this text. More precisely, this section explains how to use the TPM and its PCRs to reliably provide information about a computer's configuration.

The idea of *transitive trust* consists in trusting a *chain* of components based on a *root of trust*. A component here is a zone of memory containing executable code. Trust is said to be transitive because it passes from one component in the

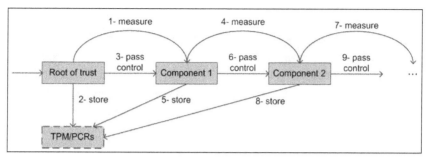

Figure 4. Establishing transitive trust.

chain to the next: the trust that can be placed in the root of trust passes to the second component in the chain; the trust in the second component passes to the third in the chain; and so on. Establishing transitive trust involves three basic steps (see Figure 4):[2]

- *measure the next component,* i.e., obtain its cryptographic hash;
- *store the measurement* by extending a PCR in the TPM; and
- *pass control to the measured component,* i.e., run the component that was measured.

The objective is to provide reliable measurements so that a challenger can assess whether the system is in a trusted state—that is, verify its integrity. If the challenger trusts the root of trust, then it can trust that the first measurement was taken correctly; if it realizes that the first measurement belongs to a trusted component, then it can trust that the second measurement was taken correctly; and so on.

Let us be even clearer about how trust is actually passed from one component to the next. Consider the root of trust: we trust it, so we trust that it measures component 1 correctly. If the measurement of component 1 corresponds to a trusted component, then we can trust component 1. Notice that there has to be some kind of list of measurements that correspond to trusted components. The process is the same for the rest of the chain: if we trust component 1, we trust that it measures component 2 correctly; if the measurement of component 2 corresponds to a trusted component, then we can trust component 2; and so on.

An example illustrates this procedure.

2   Grawrock, 2009.

The root of trust in commodity PCs with a TPM should be platform hardware that takes a measurement of the BIOS.[3] When the PC is turned on, the PCRs are set to 0. During the boot process, several modules run in sequence, each one passing control to the next one—first the BIOS, then the master boot record (MBR), the kernel, and so forth. To obtain transitive trust, each module calculates and extends one of the PCRs with the hash of the next module. This sequence of steps stores in the TPM a set of hashes that this component can provide to challengers—processes in other computers charged with verifying whether the system is in a trusted state, i.e., whether the system is running a certain version of the BIOS characterized by having a certain hash, a certain version of the MBR, etc. From a practical standpoint, notice that at least the main Linux distributions already support storing hashes in the TPM. Some security information and event management (SIEM) systems can obtain these hashes to provide information about the security state of a set of computers.

This process of assessing the security state of a computer based on the values stored in the PCRs may seem to have the following vulnerability: after booting a configuration (BIOS, MBR, kernel) that challengers do not consider trusted, what if the system modifies some of the PCRs in the TPM to hashes that the challengers trust? This would trick the challengers into believing that the configuration is the one the hashes represent, when this is not the case. However, recall that this is not possible because the TPM has no operation to write a value into a PCR—only to extend a PCR. So, instead of storing the hash provided by whatever calls the TPM in a PCR, the extension operation stores a hash of the PCR's previous value concatenated with the input hash. The PCR's previous value is 0 the first time a hash is stored, but not later. Due to the collision resistance property of cryptographic hash functions, it is impossible to extend a PCR so that its state becomes a trusted hash. This means that the TPM design itself avoids this vulnerability.

In this context the root of trust is often called the *root of trust for measurement* (RTM), as it serves to measure the platform. If the RTM is in the hardware or in the BIOS, it is called a *static* RTM (SRTM) because it is mandatorily at the beginning of the boot process, and it cannot change. The notion of *dynamic RTM* (DRTM) supported by the AMD's Secure Virtual Machine (SVM)[4] and Intel's

---

3   B. Parno, "Trust Extension for Commodity Computers," *Communications of the ACM*, vol. 55, no. 6, June 2012, pp. 76–85.

4   G. Strongin, "Trusted Computing Using AMD 'Pacifica' and 'Presidio' Secure Virtual Machine Technology," *Information Security Technical Report*, vol. 10, no. 2, Jan. 2005, pp. 120–132.

Trusted eXecution Technology (TXT),[5] two extensions to the x86 architecture, removes this limitation of the RTM being tied to the boot process.[6] The main difference between SRTM and DRTM is that the latter enables the system to start establishing transitive trust at any time, not just at boot time. For this to be possible, the extensions provide instructions to put the CPU in a clean state, akin to a restart, but from which it is possible to return to normal operation. This clean state represents a new root of trust.

5   *Intel Trusted Execution Technology (Intel TXT): Software Development Guide*, document number 315168-008, Intel, Mar. 2011; http://download.intel.com/technology/security/downloads/315168.pdf.
6   McCune et al., 2010.

Chapter 4:
Protecting Consumers' Data in the Cloud

To protect the confidentiality and integrity of data kept in the cloud, the cloud infrastructure has to prevent certain attacks and give consumers the ability to assess that this protection is in place.

The latter requirement may seem excessive, but it arises from the concern we are dealing with: the malicious insider threat. A malicious insider is in a sense part of the cloud, so he or she can provide false information to the consumer. In our solution, trust is grounded on hardware—the TPM or CPU extensions for DRTM—instead of software and cloud operators.

We now present the two protection schemes: basic (Section 4.1) and enhanced (Section 4.2).

4.1 Basic Protection

Our solution for protecting consumers' data (and applications) in the cloud is based on the assumption that the attacks against the VM come through the infrastructure, i.e., through the management VM—we assume that they do not target vulnerabilities in the consumer VMs themselves. From the lifecycle viewpoint, this assumption suggests that the consumer provides its own VM images, instead of using off-the-shelf images supplied by the cloud provider.

The solution is based on two principles:

1. in the cloud, consumer VMs are either encrypted or running in a *trusted virtualization environment* (TVE);
2. before a VM is decrypted and executed in a TVE, the consumer attests that it can trust the TVE, i.e., that the TVE is indeed a *trusted* virtual environment.

Consumer VMs reside in the cloud in three places: in VM servers, in the network (e.g., during deployment and migration), and backed up on disks. To prevent data disclosure and modification, we have to limit what a system administrator can do with a VM on a server and force it to be encrypted on the network and when backed up. Therefore, servers must run a TVE.

A *trusted virtualization environment* (TVE) is the infrastructure software that runs on a VM server. Figure 2 makes it clear that the main components of the TVE are the *hypervisor* and the *management VM*, but there are others, such as the BIOS and the MBR (see Section 3.2). The software configuration of a VM server is said to be a TVE if:

- it does not provide certain operations to administrators (such as snapshots and volume mount, which would allow the attacks presented in);[1] and
- it supports only trusted versions of certain critical operations (launch, migrate, backup, and terminate VMs).

Referring to one TVE is a simplification; cloud consumers can trust several TVE configurations.

---

1   F. Rocha and M. Correia, "Lucy in the Sky without Diamonds: Stealing Confidential Data in the Cloud," *Proc. 1st Int'l Workshop Dependability of Clouds, Data Centers and Virtual Computing Environments*, IEEE CS, June 2011, pp. 129–134.

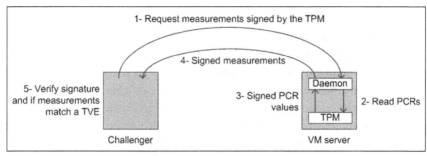

Figure 5. Remote server attestation.

A final comment before delving into the details: the basic solution builds on remote attestation based on a static root of trust for measurement (SRTM).

Remote Attestation

The consumer attests that it can trust the TVE (principle 2) by using *remote attestation*. The idea consists in verifying the configuration of the VM server by getting a set of measurements. The boot process of the VM server has to follow the transitive trust establishment process explained in Section 3.2. Therefore, the hashes of its BIOS, MBR, hypervisor, and management VM have to be stored in the PCRs in the TPM.

Figure 5 illustrates the remote attestation process for a challenging computer (left) attesting a VM server (right). For now, simply consider that the challenging computer is controlled by the consumer in some way; later we explain what this computer is.

The process is as follows: the challenger requests a vector with measurements from the VM server (1). This request is a message that is received by a daemon in the VM server, running in the management VM. This daemon requests these measurements of the TPM, i.e., the daemon asks the TPM to quote the PCRs, where the relevant measurements are stored (2). The TPM returns this quote, which is a vector that is signed using the private part of the TPM's endorsement key-pair (EK) (3). This key never leaves the TPM and uniquely identifies it. The public part of the pair is available in a certificate—signed by the TPM vendor—that attests that it is indeed the public key of an EK pair of a (real) TPM. This is important so that the challenger can know that it is contacting a real TPM, not some kind of emulator. The challenger has access to this certificate somehow (e.g., it can come in the reply). The VM server replies with the signed vector (4).

Finally, the challenger verifies the signature and checks to see whether the measurements correspond to those of a TVE (5).

The challenger has to obtain information about which TVEs it can trust, i.e., about vectors of measurements that correspond to TVEs. This information can be obtained in different ways and still be more or less reliable. The simplest solution is to trust the cloud provider and obtain certificates with known-good measurements from it using some kind of media that cannot be tampered with by a malicious insider. A solution for consumers with high security requirements could be—in the future—to obtain these hashes from an independent laboratory that evaluates the involved software components, comparable to the Common Criteria evaluation (www.commoncriteriaportal.org).

Critical Management Operations

Remote attestation is essential to assure the consumer that its VM is running in a TVE. However, we need to understand when this operation is executed during the lifecycle of a VM. More specifically, we need to discuss how it relates to four important operations done to VMs:

- VM launching—in a server;
- VM migration—to a different server;
- VM backup—to storage;
- VM termination—removal from the cloud.

These are the VM operations that we identified as critical for security. There may be others, but we believe they will be protected in a way that is similar to these four.

To explain these operations we need to introduce a few abstract components that we call *agents* (see Figure 6). An operation is requested by the *consumer agent*, a software component controlled by the consumer. That component can contact the *management agent* that is part of the *administration frontend* (see Figure 3). There are other management agents in the VM controller, in the service controller, and possibly in other parts of the cloud infrastructure. There are also *server agents* in the management VM of the servers. The consumer owns and therefore trusts the consumer agent. It also trusts the server agent after remotely attesting it. It cannot trust either the management agents or the rest of the cloud infrastructure.

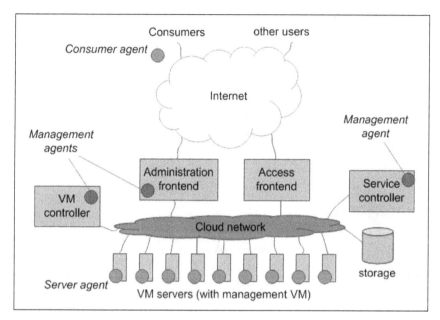

Figure 6. Cloud architecture with consumer, management, and server agents represented.

VM Launching

Our solution is based on the principle that consumer VMs run in a TVE. Therefore, the operation of launching a VM is critical because it must be launched in a TVE. This section explains how this requirement is enforced. The basic idea consists in the consumer performing remote attestation of the server where the VM is instantiated.

Figure 7 represents the operation of launching a VM. The consumer agent, which is trusted, contacts a management agent in the administration frontend to request that the VM be instantiated (1). This agent, which is not trusted, possibly after contacting other management agents, also not trusted, replies to the consumer agent with the address of the server agent of the server where the VM will be instantiated, e.g., an IP address plus a port number (2). One of the management agents requests that the server agent launch the VM (3). The consumer agent contacts the server agent to do remote attestation of the server (4) and receives the signed measurements that it uses to verify that it can trust the server (5). If it turns out the server can be trusted—i.e., if the consumer agent considers

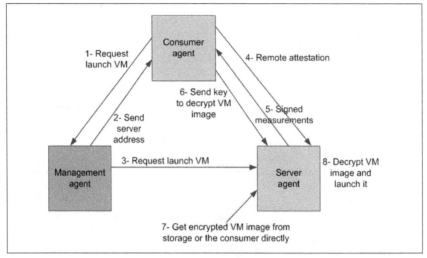

Figure 7. VM launching operation.

the server configuration a TVE—the consumer agent sends the server agent a key to decrypt the VM image using a secure channel (e.g., SSL/TLS) (6), and the server agent gets the VM image from some storage service inside the cloud itself or directly from the consumer (7). Finally, the server agent decrypts the VM image and launches a new VM with that image (8).

As described, the VM launching operation has two limitations:

- it involves putting a computer outside the cloud in the loop of control operations (VM launching, but also other operations, as we will see);
- it involves giving consumers information about the internals of the cloud—node identity, software configuration—something that cloud providers are not interested in doing.

To solve these problems there are two alternative implementations of the operation. The first consists in the challenger being a VM of the customer, running in the cloud. This VM itself needs to be attested by the consumer agent, but this is not an excessive burden if the consumer runs many VMs in the cloud. This solution solves the first problem, but not the second.

Another alternative—the best one—has the challenger belong to the cloud provider. Such a challenger is under the control of the cloud provider, so it is po-

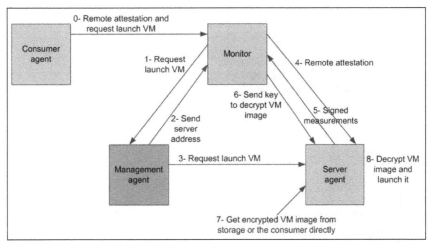

Figure 8. VM launching operation with monitor.

tentially reachable by a malicious insider. Therefore, it has to be remotely attested by a second challenger, which resides in the facilities of the consumer. Santos et al. have advocated this solution and shown that it is practical.[2] Figure 8 shows the VM launching operation with this new component, called the *monitor*. This component essentially takes on the role of the consumer agent in Figure 7. The consumer agent here just does remote attestation of the monitor and requests launching the VM (step 0). The consumer agent is no longer in the loop of the operation.

VM Migration

It has been shown that instantiating a VM in a TVE is not enough to protect it because of the following potential attack: at first, the VM is instantiated in a TVE so it is protected; however, once instantiated it is migrated to a different VM server that is not a TVE; therefore, it comes to be at the mercy of the attacker.[3]

2   Santos et al., 2012.

3   N. Santos, K.P. Gummadi, and R. Rodrigues, "Towards Trusted Cloud Computing," *Proc. 1st Workshop Hot Topics in Cloud Computing* (HotCloud 09), USENIX, 2009; http://static. usenix.org/event/hotcloud09/tech/full_papers/santos.pdf.

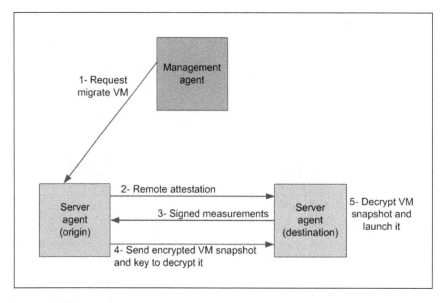

Figure 9. VM migration operation.

Recall the beginning of Section 4.1: a TVE does not provide certain operations and only provides trusted versions of certain others. This is exactly the case with VM migration because preventing the aforementioned attack requires:

- providing a *trusted VM migration operation* that ensures that the destination server is also a TVE; this secure VM migration operation is what we present in this section;
- preventing any other functionality of the TVE from allowing a VM to be migrated to a different server; this is a requirement for a TVE to be considered trusted.

Figure 9 represents an execution of the VM migration operation. This operation can be triggered by several events: explicitly by the consumer, due to a maintenance operation in the cloud, etc. The triggering event is not represented in the figure.

The first step consists of the management agent requesting the migration from the server agent of the server where the VM is running (1). This request takes the address of the destination server. The origin server agent is trusted because it was remotely attested either by the consumer when the VM was launched (as in the

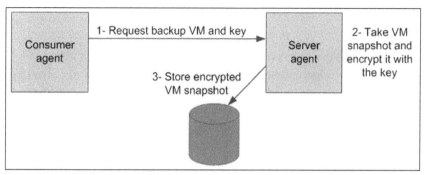

Figure 10. VM backup operation.

previous section) or in a VM migration operation like the one we are presenting. This trusted server agent does remote attestation of the destination server agent (2, 3). If this attestation is successful, the destination server agent is a TVE. If that is the case, the operation continues with the origin server agent sending a snapshot of the VM memory plus some state information (e.g., the content of CPU registers, such as the instruction pointer (IP)) encrypted using a symmetric encryption algorithm (e.g., AES) to the destination server agent (4). The figure mentions that the decryption key has also to be sent; the obvious way to send it is to create a secure channel between the two agents and send the VM snapshot encrypted with the session key. The destination server agent decrypts and launches the VM.

Notice that VM migration can be more complicated than simply sending such a snapshot. To minimize the time it is stopped, it can be sent in several phases: first memory pages that are not being used are sent, then control is passed to the destination server, and finally, the rest of the pages are sent.[4] However, the idea remains the same: there is data that describes the content and state of the VM that has to be sent encrypted between the two servers.

Notice that the consumer agent is not involved in the operation, so there is no computer outside the cloud in the loop of this operation.

4   C. Clark et al., "Live Migration of Virtual Machines," *Proc. 2nd Symp. Networked Systems Design and Implementation*, USENIX, May 2005, pp. 273–286.

VM Backup

Backing up data is a common mechanism to allow for recovery in case data gets corrupted or lost. Virtualization allows extending this mechanism to the code and the state of the (virtual) machine. In the cloud VMs can be backed up on the initiative of the cloud itself or on that of the consumer, e.g., to release resources when they are not needed. In both cases the backed up VM is essentially a memory snapshot whose content can be easily analyzed. The solution is basically to encrypt the VM snapshot before it is backed up.

Figure 10 represents the VM backup operation in the case in which the consumer starts it. The consumer agent requests the operation and provides a key to encrypt it using a symmetric encryption algorithm, e.g., AES (1). Then the server agent takes a snapshot of the VM plus some state (as in VM migration) and encrypts it with the key provided by the consumer agent (2). Finally, the server agent sends the VM snapshot to the backup medium, e.g., to a cloud storage service, and destroys the key (3).

Notice that no remote attestation is needed because the TVE where the server agent is running has already been attested either when the VM was first instantiated with the VM launching operation or when the VM was migrated to its current server using the VM migration operation.

VM Termination

VM termination is not a particularly problematic operation, except for the fact that it can leave confidential data in the memory or disk of the server where the VM was running. To disclose this information, a malicious insider would simply access that memory or disk space after the VM was terminated. A malicious consumer might also launch VMs in several servers in order to explore and find confidential data in recently released memory and disk spaces.

The solution is simply to clean (set to zero) the memory and disk space used when a VM is terminated. No remote attestation is needed for the same reason as for the VM backup operation. We do not present a figure due to the simplicity of the solution.

4.2 Enhanced Protection

The basic protection solution presented in Section 4.1 is a great advancement in relation to a standard cloud infrastructure: it provides consumers assurance that their VMs are either running in a TVE or are encrypted. Furthermore, consumers can have some assurance that TVEs provide a set of reliable operations (VM launching, migration, etc.). However, the basic solution has two limitations:

1. Remote attestation can consider trusted a configuration that is actually not trustworthy. A TVE contains a hypervisor, the management VM, and other modules, which means that it can easily total hundreds of thousand lines of code.[5] Such a large module is likely to contain vulnerabilities (e.g., buffer-overflow, command-injection, format-string vulnerabilities) that would let an attacker subvert its normal functioning (e.g., by injecting arbitrary code into the VM).

2. A TPM can only perform around two signatures per second, so it can easily become a bottleneck if there are many operations that involve remote attestation, i.e., VM launching and VM migration operations.

These two limitations derive from the use of a *static root of trust for measurement* (SRTM). The first limitation is linked to the need for attesting the platform components starting from the SRTM. The second is due to the need for using the TPM for attestation based on the SRTM.

The solution to these two limitations consists in exploiting a *dynamic root of trust for measurement* (DRTM). The number of vulnerabilities in software is believed to be proportional to its size, so reducing the attested code size is an important goal. The use of a DRTM makes this possible: it can help prove to cloud consumers that the modules responsible for launching, migrating, or destroying their VMs are trustworthy. Furthermore, it can do so while using the TPM less frequently.

Our solution is based on one of the few existing efficient DRTM-based mechanisms: TrustVisor. Note, however, that TrustVisor is still a research prototype, which means that implementing the enhanced protection will necessarily be harder to carry out than the basic protection, at this stage. A prototype of TrustVisor is currently available as part of the eXtensible Modular Hypervisor Framework (http://sourceforge.net/projects/xmhf).

---

5   Steinberg and Kauer, 2010.

DRTM and TrustVisor

The term trusted computing base (TCB) denotes all elements "responsible for supporting the security policy and supporting the isolation of objects" in a system.[6] TrustVisor[7] is a special purpose hypervisor that takes advantage of a DRTM to minimize its TCB and builds on this small TCB to enforce code and execution integrity, as well as data integrity and secrecy, for selected parts of an application. In TrustVisor lingo, these parts of an application are called *pieces of application logic* (PALs).

TrustVisor provides an isolated execution environment (IEE) for PALs, which addresses the first limitation we aim to solve. To ensure memory protection, TrustVisor uses hardware and operation modes. TrustVisor uses current hardware support (e.g., 2D hardware page walkers and IOMMU) to provide strong isolation for PALs from legacy operating systems and from DMA-capable devices. A system controlled through TrustVisor has three basic operation modes. First, the *host mode*, in which TrustVisor itself has control of the platform. Second, the *legacy guest mode*, where the legacy OS and its applications execute. Finally, the PALs execute in isolation from the legacy OS and its applications in the *secure guest mode*.

To grant protection through TrustVisor's security mechanisms, the application developer must first register the PAL(s). A *micro* TPM (μTPM) is associated with each PAL upon registration. A μTPM is contained within TrustVisor's TCB and provides functionality that is similar to the TPM but implemented in software. This registration allows TrustVisor to distinguish between PALs and legacy OSs and applications. After registration, when a PAL needs to execute TrustVisor it uses a DRTM-like mechanism denominated *TrustVisor root of trust for measurement* (TRTM) to start an IEE. The TRTM provides a known-good initial state, memory protection from DMA access, and integrity measurement of the PAL's code before execution. TRTM can be trusted because TrustVisor's TCB is small enough to be trustworthy.

An important feature of TrustVisor is its *two-level integrity measurement*. TrustVisor is started and measured using DRTM-based mechanisms (e.g., the

---

6   Department of Defense, *Trusted Computer System Evaluation Criteria*, DoD 5200.28-STD, Dec. 1985.

7   McCune et al., 2010.

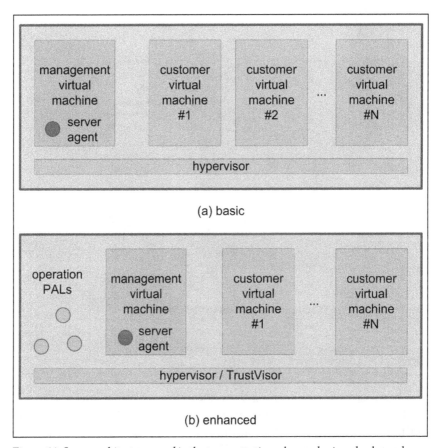

Figure 11. Server architectures used in the two protection schemes: basic and enhanced.

SKINIT instruction of AMD CPUs), and its measurements are stored in the platform's physical TPM. However, each PAL has its own µTPM, which it uses to perform and store measurements. The storing capacity is offered through micro PCRs (µPCRs). There is no risk of data leakage because TrustVisor zeroes the memory region where this information is kept when a PAL terminates. This approach removes the TPM from attestations performed during runtime, which is important because TPM operations are slow—this addresses the second limitation we aim to solve with TrustVisor/DRTM.

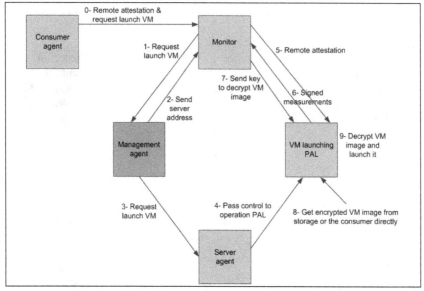

Figure 12. Enhanced VM launching operation (with monitor).

Critical Management Operations

The basic idea of implementing the critical management operations with a DRTM is to make the code of each operation a TrustVisor PAL. Therefore, there will be four *operation PALs*: VM launching, VM migration, VM backup, and VM termination. Using TrustVisor and a DRTM, we manage to achieve interesting properties that solve the limitations of the basic protection solution:

- trust in a small component, because the system will attest the four operation PALs;
- fast attestation, because attestation will be handled by the μTPMs.

Notice that when a PAL is remotely attested using a μTPM the TVE is also attested due to the two-level integrity measurement feature of TrustVisor. This is important because when launching or migrating a VM the consumer needs to be assured that the management VM does not provide dangerous functionality. On the negative side, we still trust the TVE—which is large—not to provide such dangerous operations. This is a limitation of our solution, but one that can be managed with some of the techniques to reduce the size of the TCB discussed in Section 5.3.

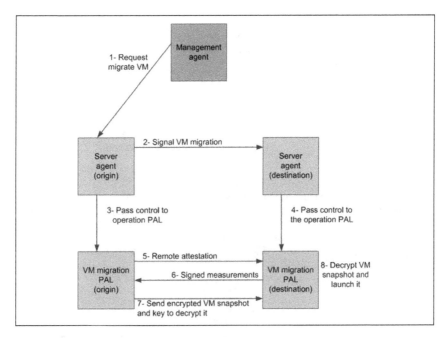

Figure 13. Enhanced VM migration operation.

Figure 11 compares the server architecture used in the basic protection scheme (Figure 2 and Section 4.1) and the architecture used in the enhanced protection scheme (this section).

We now present the versions of the four critical operations of the enhanced protection scheme.

VM Launching and Migration

The enhanced versions of the VM launching and migration operations are presented respectively in Figures 12 and 13. A comparison of these two figures with Figures 6 and 7 shows that there are the following differences:

- there is a new component involved, the PAL of the operation;
- the role of the server agent is mostly to pass control to the PAL;
- the PAL is the component that actually executes the operation;
- it is the PAL that is remotely attested.

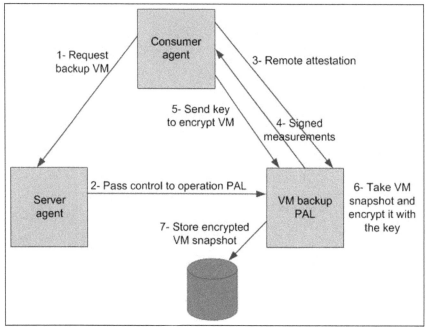

Figure 14. Enhanced VM backup operation.

VM Backup and Termination

Unlike the operations of the previous section, the basic versions of VM backup and VM termination do not involve attestation. However, the use of a DRTM and TrustVisor implies doing attestation; therefore, these operations change more than the other two.

Figure 14 shows the new version of the VM backup operation. In comparison to Figure 10 that presented the basic version, there is one more component—the VM backup PAL—but also more interaction between the consumer agent and the cloud, due to the need to perform remote attestation. For the rest of the operation, the idea is similar to the two previous: it is now the PAL that runs the actual operation—in this case, backing up the VM.

The VM termination operation changes in a similar way to VM backup. We do not present a figure because it would be very similar to Figure 14. The differences would be that steps 5 and 7 would disappear, and step 6 would be the termination and the cleaning of the memory space and disk.

Chapter 5:
Related Work

T his chapter goes over related literature without trying to be exhaustive. First, it presents two alternative approaches to the problem we are concerned with here—homomorphic encryption and intrusion tolerance/ Byzantine fault tolerance—and discusses why they fail to solve it. Second, it discusses work that reduces the size of the TCB, which is an important technique, complementary to our approach, as we have to ensure that the TVE does not provide dangerous functionality. Finally, it gives an overview of work on approaches closely related to the one we follow.

5.1 Homomorphic Encryption

We are interested in the confidentiality and integrity of consumer data kept in the cloud. If we considered only confidentiality, encryption would be the obvious mechanism to enforce it. Although we also consider integrity, let us discuss just the use of encryption in this context.

Data kept in an IaaS cloud that runs VMs for consumers cannot be simply encrypted. Consider what data is in such an environment: files, web pages, variables, data structures, databases, etc. Consider also how consumers use an IaaS cloud: they run application servers (JBoss, Glassfish, etc.), MapReduce jobs, etc. To encrypt data in such formats and manipulated by such applications, the applications themselves would have to be extensively modified. Modifying such applications is not necessarily impossible, but it certainly is complicated.

Moreover, these applications manipulate the data: they analyze it, perform algebraic operations on it, make control flow decisions depending on its content, and so on. If the data is encrypted this is typically not possible. However, *fully homomorphic encryption* (FHE) has appeared recently as a solution to this difficulty.[1] An FHE scheme allows the computing of an arbitrary function over encrypted data. Nevertheless, the current performance of FHE seems to make it infeasible for protecting the consumer data used, e.g., in application servers in the cloud. One solution is to improve the performance of FHE, which is a current topic of research.

An alternative solution to the bad performance of FHE is to use a combination of *homomorphic encryption* (HE) schemes that are not fully homomorphic, i.e., that individually do not allow computing arbitrary functions over the encrypted data. Popa et al. use this idea to perform encrypted queries in a database management system called CryptDB.[2] The solution is more intricate than if FHE had been used, but the performance is arguably sufficient for many applications.

Yet another solution is the use of a *somewhat homomorphic encryption* (SwHE) scheme, i.e., a scheme that allows a fixed number of multiplications of ciphertext, but not arbitrary computation. Lauter et al. have shown that their implementation of an SwHE scheme is efficient enough for several applications.[3]

Using FHE, HE, or SwHE schemes has a difficulty that makes it incompatible with many cloud applications, at least at the current state of knowledge. Cloud computing is commonly used by consumers to provide services to external us-

---

1   C. Gentry, "Fully Homomorphic Encryption Using Ideal Lattices," *Proc. 41st ACM Ann. Symp. Theory Computing* (STOC 09), ACM, 2009, pp. 169–178.
2   R.A. Popa et al., "CryptDB: Protecting Confidentiality with Encrypted Query Processing," *Proc. 23rd ACM Symp. Operating Systems Principles* (SOSP 2011), ACM, Oct. 2011, pp. 85–100.
3   K. Lauter, Naehrig, and V. Vaikuntanathan, "Can Homomorphic Encryption be Practical?," *Proc. 3rd ACM Cloud Computing Security Workshop* (CCSW 11), ACM, Oct. 2011, pp. 113–124.

ers. However, if these users are meant to access data processed using FHE, HE, or SwHE, they have to have access to the encryption keys. This is certainly feasible if external users are just a few and are highly trusted, but not in the general case, e.g., if the service is intended to be used openly. This is even more true if these users' data is stored and processed in the cloud. This observation was formalized by van Dijk and Juels based on three classes of cloud computing applications: private single-client computing, private multiclient computing, and stateful private multiclient computing.[4]

5.2 Intrusion Tolerance/Byzantine Fault Tolerance

The approach proposed in this book has to be implemented *by the cloud provider.* This section is about an approach that can be implemented *by the consumer* that is transparent to the cloud provider. In a sense implementing these mechanisms can be an extra burden, but they also empower the consumer to deal with the issue independently from the cooperation of the cloud provider.

Fault tolerance has been studied for decades in the more general context of dependability.[5] The approach consists basically in accepting that faults (e.g., crashes, corrupted messages) are inevitable and in enhancing the system with mechanisms to tolerate these faults (i.e., to mask their effects or to detect and recover from them).

Fault tolerance typically deals with accidental faults, but in the last decade or so the tolerance of *malicious faults* under the designation of *intrusion tolerance*[6] or *Byzantine fault tolerance*[7] has also been thoroughly studied. An intrusion-tolerant or Byzantine fault-tolerant (BFT) system can tolerate that some of its components misbehave for intentional or malicious reasons, which obviously includes misbehavior caused by a malicious insider.[8]

---

4   M. van Dijk and A. Juels, "On the Impossibility of Cryptography Alone for Privacy-Preserving Cloud Computing," *Proc. 5th USENIX Conf. Hot Topics in Security,* USENIX, 2010, pp. 1–8.

5   A. Avizienis et al., "Basic concepts and taxonomy of dependable and secure computing," *IEEE Trans. Dependable and Secure Computing,* vol. 1, no. 1, Mar. 2004, pp. 11–33.

6   J.S. Fraga and D. Powell, "A fault- and intrusion-tolerant file system," *Proc. 3rd IFIP Int'l Conf. Computer Security,* Aug. 1985, pp. 203–218.

7   L. Lamport, R. Shostak, and M. Pease, "The Byzantine generals problem," *ACM Trans. Programming Languages and Systems,* vol. 4, no. 3, July 1982, pp. 382–401.

8   A survey of the area can be found in P. Verissimo et al., "Intrusion-Resilient Middleware Design and Validation," *Information Assurance, Security and Privacy Services,* H. Raghav Rao and

We now discuss to what extent this approach solves the problem we are interested in:

1. if used in a way that is generic enough to implement something close to IaaS, it does not ensure confidentiality, only integrity (plus availability);
2. if used to implement only data storage, losing generality, it can be used to obtain both integrity and confidentiality (plus availability).

Let us consider the first case: providing generality without confidentiality. This case is made possible through a technique called *state machine replication*, first implemented efficiently with BFT by Castro and Liskov.[9] The idea is as follows: a certain service is replicated in a few servers; all replicas start in the same state; replica state is only modified by commands issued by clients; commands are deterministic, so they modify the state equally in all replicas; all commands are executed in the same order by all servers, thanks to a total order broadcast protocol; given this ordering, all replicas that are not faulty give the same replies to clients, so clients can compare the replies they get and choose the majority reply (the approach assumes the majority is not faulty). This provides integrity because a faulty replica cannot compromise the state as seen by the client. The approach also provides availability because the system remains operational even if some of the replicas fail. It does nothing to provide confidentiality, which in a sense becomes worse because data is kept in all replicas. Data might be encrypted using the techniques of Section 5.1, with the limitations we discussed.

This idea can be exploited in the context of cloud computing by putting a replica in a separate cloud, an idea that to the best of our knowledge has not yet been fully explored, although it is being investigated. For IaaS what would be replicated would be a VM, but VMs are not deterministic and have intricate interactions with the hypervisor and the hardware, so this is far from simple. More feasible would be to put a replica of the application in each cloud, assuming it has a simpler interface with the outside world.

The opposite idea—obtaining integrity and confidentiality without generality—has been explored to a far greater degree in the context of cloud computing.

Shambhu Upadhyaya, eds., Emerald, 2009, pp. 615–678.
9   M. Castro and B. Liskov, "Practical Byzantine Fault Tolerance," *Proc. 3rd Symp. Operating Systems Design and Implementation* (OSDI 99), USENIX, 1999, pp. 173–186.

DepSky is a system that aims to guarantee confidentiality, integrity, and availability of data stored in the cloud.[10] DepSky does not provide the IaaS model, but only a storage service similar, for example, to Amazon S3. DepSky replicates data across several storage clouds assigned to different cloud providers, e.g., four of them. It uses Byzantine quorum system algorithms to assure the integrity and availability of data, even in the presence of failure, data loss, or corruption in some of the clouds. The confidentiality of the data is assured by encrypting it and storing the encryption key in all the clouds using secret sharing. This solution allows the implementation of secure storage clouds but does not protect data in IaaS clouds that provide VMs to the user. The HAIL system also uses several storage clouds to provide integrity and availability of data stored in the cloud.[11] HAIL employs erasure codes and cryptographic techniques such as proofs of retrievability (PORs) that give assurance that a certain file is stored in the cloud and not corrupted.

Both DepSky and HAIL build trust on top of a set of untrusted clouds. There are other systems that build trust on top of a single untrusted cloud. FAUST[12] and Depot[13] ensure the integrity of data stored in an untrusted cloud, but not its availability or confidentiality. These systems are based on the notion of fork consistency. Kamara and Lauter present a scheme with similar objectives but that manages to provide data confidentiality by exploiting a set of cryptographic primitives.[14] A drawback of their scheme is that it involves communication between who stores data in the cloud and who reads it. All these systems and schemes require that the cloud runs code that is specific to the system/scheme, as opposed to DepSky that uses storage clouds as building blocks (all the DepSky code is at the client).

Table 2 compares these techniques with those of the previous section in terms of properties that they can provide, the entity that is protected, and the limitations of each technique in comparison to the approach we use in this text.

---

10   Bessani et al., 2011.

11   Bowers, Juels, and Oprea, 2009.

12   C. Cachin, I. Keidar, and A. Shraer, "Fail-Aware Untrusted Storage," *Proc. 39th IEEE/IFIP Int'l Conf. Dependable Systems and Networks* (DSN 09), IEEE CS, 2009, pp. 494–503.

13   P. Mahajan et al., "Depot: Cloud Storage with Minimal Trust," *Proc. 9th USENIX Symp. Operating Systems Design and Implementation* (OSDI 10), USENIX, Oct. 2010, pp. 307–322.

14   S. Kamara and K. Lauter, "Cryptographic Cloud Storage," *Proc. 14th Int'l Conf. Financial Cryptography and Data Security*, 2010, pp. 136–149.

Table 2. Comparison of encryption and intrusion tolerance/Byzantine fault tolerance techniques.

	Technique	Property it can provide			Entity protected	Limitation	References
		Confiden-tiality	Integrity	Avail-ability			
Encryption	Homomorphic encryption	Yes	No	No	VMs	Must change application	Gentry, 2009. Popa et al, 2011. Lauter, Naehrig, and Vaikuntanathan, 2011.
IntTol/BFT	State machine replication	No	Yes	Yes	Application, maybe VMs	Confidentiality missing	Castro and Liskov, 1999.
	Storage in a few clouds	Yes	Yes	Yes	Storage only	Storage only	Bessani et al, 2011. Bowers, Juels, and Oprea, 2009.
	Storage in a single cloud	Yes	Yes	No	Storage only	Storage only	Cachin, Keidar, and Shraer, 2009. Mahajan et al., 2010. Kamara and Lauter, 2010.

Notice that the works in the references do not necessarily provide all the properties that the technique *can* provide (e.g., Cachin, Keidar, and Shraer do not provide confidentiality).

5.3 Reducing the Size of the TCB

Much early research used to assume that hypervisors are thin layers that provide isolation between VMs and are protected from them, therefore constituting the perfect tools for implementing a variety of security mechanisms. However, in recent years the research community has started to understand that the trusted computing base (TCB) in such virtualized environments is quite large, in the order of hundreds of thousands of lines of code, so hypervisors may provide a root for security that is weaker than previously thought.[15]

Murray et al. understood that "the management of a Xen-based system requires a privileged, full-blown operating system to be included in the trusted computing base."[16] This operating system is essentially Xen's Dom0, which corresponds to the management VM of Figure 2. Their proposal is to *disaggregate* a Xen-based system, i.e., to move some core Dom0 functionality to a trusted VM that runs alongside Dom0. This approach reduces the TCB to the hypervisor plus that trusted VM.

NOVA is a different solution to the same problem.[17] It is a *virtualization architecture* designed from scratch with the purpose of reducing the TCB in virtualized systems. A core principle is the fine-grained functional decomposition of the virtualization layer. This layer is decomposed into a microhypervisor, the root partition manager, multiple virtual machine monitors (which are distinct from the hypervisor in NOVA), device drivers, and other services. The second core principle is the enforcement of the least privilege principle among these layers. NOVA reduces the size of the TCB by at least one order of magnitude.

These two works are not specifically about virtualization for cloud computing, but the ones we describe for the remainder of this section are.

Xoar breaks the virtualization layer into several modules, as in NOVA, but it is based on Xen, not built from scratch.[18] Xoar disaggregates the management VM into single-purpose components called *service VMs*. These components can be shared or not between consumer VMs, allowing different security policies.

---

15 An interesting comparison of the size of several hypervisors can be found in Steinberg and Kauer, 2010.

16 Murray, Milos, and Hand, 2008.

17 Steinberg and Kauer, 2010.

18 P. Colp et al., "Breaking Up is Hard to Do: Security and Functionality in a Commodity Hypervisor," *Proc. 23rd ACM Symp. Operating Systems Principles* (SOSP 11), ACM, Oct. 2011, pp. 189–202.

The NoHype system is a radically different solution for the same problem.[19] It is also based on Xen, but it manages to run VMs *natively* on top of the hardware, thereby for the most part removing the hypervisor from the attack surface of the system.

Min-V takes a simpler and easier to implement approach.[20] Virtualization systems use many virtual devices (for example, 39 in Hyper-V): graphic card, serial port, DVD/CD-ROM, keyboard, etc. Min-V does two things: it disables virtual devices that are not needed when virtualization is used in the cloud, and for the remaining virtual devices it removes all functionality not needed in the cloud. In a sense, Min-V explores the intrinsic modularity of such systems for disaggregation.

There is also related work on hardening the hypervisor against attacks. For instance, HyperSafe protects hypervisors from control-flow hijacking attacks (e.g., buffer overflows, format string attacks, command injection).[21]

5.4 Related Approaches

This section presents work that is closely related to the approach we have described herein. It presents work on trusted computing as a mechanism for securing both virtualization and cloud computing.

In this book we use trusted computing technologies such as the TPM as mechanisms for "bootstrapping trust" in servers, i.e., for measuring their security state and for remotely attesting them. There was a great deal of work in this area for a few decades, but a recent book does a very good job summarizing it.[22]

Our enhanced approach involves starting an isolated execution environment based on a DRTM. We propose using TrustVisor for this purpose, so we presented it in Section 4.2. Another system, SICE, evolves these ideas but is con-

---

19 J. Szefer et al., "Eliminating the Hypervisor Attack Surface for a More Secure Cloud," *Proc. 18th ACM Conf. Computer and Communications Security* (CCS 2011), ACM, Oct. 2011, pp. 401–412.

20 A. Nguyen et al., "Delusional Boot: Securing Cloud Hypervisors without Massive Re-engineering," *Proc. European Conf. Computer Systems* (EuroSys 12), Apr. 2012, pp. 141–154.

21 Z. Wang and X. Jiang, "HyperSafe: A lightweight approach to provide lifetime hypervisor control-flow integrity," *Proc. IEEE Symp. Security and Privacy*, IEEE CS, May 2010, pp. 380–395.

22 B. Parno, J.M. McCune, and A. Perrig, *Bootstrapping Trust in Modern Computers*, Springer, 2011. Another fundamental book on trusted computing is Grawrock, 2009.

cerned with creating an IEE in multicore computers.[23] SICE builds not only on the TPM, the BIOS, and the AMD CPU, but also on the System Management Mode of the CPU.

The IBM *trusted virtual datacenter* (TVDc) technology aims to create a virtual LAN of VMs in a datacenter.[24] It builds on the IBM *hypervisor security architecture* (sHype) that implements mandatory access control in communication between VMs and intra-VM. TVDc does attestation based on the TPM and an SRTM. A similar work developed in parallel builds on the notion of *trusted virtual domains* (TVDs).[25] Security policies are not restricted to the creation of VLANs but can also include other aspects such as storage and TVD membership.

These works were not about cloud computing. Now we shift gears and discuss work specifically on trusted computing for the cloud.

Santos et al. proposed the idea of performing remote attestation of TVEs in the context of IaaS cloud computing, which is similar to our basic protection scheme.[26] Moreover, that work had the important role of identifying the VM migration attack that we mentioned when first presenting that operation in Section 4.1. Recently the same authors presented Excalibur, a full-fledged version of their system, which includes the *monitor* component explored in Section 4.1.[27] Their system is based on the notion of *policy-sealed data*, i.e., of data that is unsealed (decrypted) only in servers that satisfy certain security policies.

CloudVisor[28] is also closely related to the problem that we handle here. CloudVisor is a small security monitor that is also a hypervisor. It is inserted transparently below a commodity hypervisor, Xen. This architecture of a hypervisor below another hypervisor is an implementation of the notion of nested virtualization. The system uses both the TPM and Intel TXT to measure the configuration of the system. CloudVisor intercepts transfers of control between VMs and the commodity hypervisor. To protect consumer VM memory from

23 A.M. Azab, P. Ning, and X. Zhang, "SICE: A Hardware-Level Strongly Isolated Computing Environment for x86 Multi-core Platforms," *Proc. 18th ACM Conf. Computer and Communications Security* (CCS 11), ACM, 2011, pp. 375–388.

24 S. Berger et al., "TVDc: Managing Security in the Trusted Virtual Datacenter," *SIGOPS Operating Systems Review*, vol. 42, no. 1, Jan. 2008, pp. 40–47.

25 S. Cabuk et al., "Towards Automated Security Policy Enforcement in Multi-Tenant Virtual Data Centers," *J. Computer Security*, vol. 18, no. 1, Jan. 2010, pp. 89–121.

26 Santos, Gummadi, and Rodrigues, 2009.

27 Santos et al., 2012.

28 Zhang et al., 2011.

inspection, CloudVisor encrypts pages on the fly if it is the hypervisor that is trying to read them. CloudVisor keeps consumer files encrypted and decrypts them when they are accessed by their owner.

BoneFides is another system that allows the cloud consumer to do remote attestation based on the TPM of components of the cloud that are relevant to security.[29] However, it allows this attestation to be done in runtime, not only at VM startup, and includes protection from denial of service attacks.

The myTrustedCloud project integrates trusted computing mechanisms in Eucalyptus.[30] It allows the consumer to attest VMs, node controllers, and storage controllers (see Section 2.2) based on the TPM.

29   R. Neisse, D. Holling, and A. Pretschner, "Implementing Trust in Cloud Infrastructures," *Proc. 11th IEEE/ACM Int'l Symp. Cluster, Cloud and Grid Computing* (CCGRID), IEEE CS, May 2011, pp. 524–533.
30   D. Wallom et al., "myTrustedCloud: Trusted Cloud Infrastructure for Security-critical Computation and Data Management," *Proc. 3rd IEEE Int'l. Conf. Cloud Computing Technology and Science* (CloudCom 11), IEEE CS, 2011, pp. 247–254.

Chapter 6:
Conclusion

This text shows how to use trusted computing technologies to protect consumer data from malicious insiders in cloud computing, namely in IaaS cloud offerings. We have argued that in current offerings the consumers' data is at the mercy of such adversaries and that its confidentiality and integrity can be compromised.

An important aspect of this work is that our protection schemes are to be employed by cloud providers, not by cloud consumers. They can be used by providers to add value to their offerings. To simplify adoption, we have presented two protection schemes: basic and enhanced. The first can be implemented almost out of the box with currently available technology, while the second is based on technology that is presently only available as research prototypes.

The approach we propose has one limitation: the gap between a measurement (a hash) and a complex software module's functionality. Checking that a hash belongs to a list of trusted hashes is trivial, but actually trusting that a hash represents a trustworthy complex module is quite different. This is particularly true for vulnerabilities in hypervisors or anomalies in virtualization that can allow a malicious consumer VM to attack another one.[1] Techniques that reduce the size of the TCB have an important role to play, but they are not available for immediate use.

Another difficulty may be the management of such a solution in a production environment. Different companies will develop different software modules, and various evaluation organizations will evaluate and certify the modules, measurements, and cloud providers. All these organizations have to cooperate effectively under the pressure of a short time-to-market constraint. An additional issue is updating the measurements and revoking those that correspond to modules that eventually become untrusted.

Although we have focused here on reinforcing the cloud infrastructure with trusted computing mechanisms, we also discussed alternatives that put the burden of protecting data on the consumer. We have discussed the use of homomorphic encryption and intrusion tolerance/Byzantine fault tolerance. However, we have also shown that these solutions are not so generic and can be complicated to implement, involving, for instance, the extensive modification of the application. Nevertheless, for specific applications some of these technologies may be practical.

---

1   T. Ristenpart et al., "Hey, You, Get Off of My Cloud: Exploring Information Leakage in Third-Party Compute Clouds," *Proc. 16th ACM Conf. Computer and Communications Security*, ACM, 2009, pp. 199–212.

References

D. Abts and B. Felderman, "A Guided Tour of Data-Center Networking," *Communications of the ACM*, vol. 55, no. 6, June 2012, pp. 44–51.

A. Avizienis et al., "Basic concepts and taxonomy of dependable and secure computing," *IEEE Trans. Dependable and Secure Computing*, vol. 1, no. 1, Mar. 2004, pp. 11–33.

A.M. Azab, P. Ning, and X. Zhang, "SICE: A Hardware-Level Strongly Isolated Computing Environment for x86 Multi-core Platforms," *Proc. 18th ACM Conf. Computer and Communications Security* (CCS 11), ACM, 2011, pp. 375–388.

S. Berger et al., "TVDc: Managing Security in the Trusted Virtual Datacenter," *SIGOPS Operating Systems Review*, vol. 42, no. 1, Jan. 2008, pp. 40–47.

A. Bessani et al., "DepSky: Dependable and Secure Storage in a Cloud-of-Clouds," *Proc. European Conf. Computer Systems* (EuroSys 11), ACM, 2011, pp. 31–46.

K.D. Bowers, A. Juels, and A. Oprea, "HAIL: a High-Availability and Integrity Layer for Cloud Storage," *Proc. 16th ACM Conf. Computer and Communications Security* (CCS 09), ACM, 2009, pp. 187–198.

G. Brunette and R. Mogull, eds., *Security Guidance for Critical Areas of Focus in Cloud Computing V2.1*, Cloud Security Alliance, 2009.

S. Bugiel et al., "AmazonIA: When Elasticity Snaps Back," *Proc. 18th ACM Conf. Computer and Communications Security* (CCS 11), ACM, Oct. 2011, pp. 389–400.

S. Cabuk et al., "Towards Automated Security Policy Enforcement in Multi-Tenant Virtual Data Centers," *J. Computer Security*, vol. 18, no. 1, Jan. 2010, pp. 89–121.

C. Cachin, I. Keidar, and A. Shraer, "Fail-Aware Untrusted Storage," *Proc. 39th IEEE/IFIP Int'l Conf. Dependable Systems and Networks* (DSN 09), IEEE CS, 2009, pp. 494–503.

M. Castro and B. Liskov, "Practical Byzantine Fault Tolerance," *Proc. 3rd Symp. Operating Systems Design and Implementation* (OSDI 99), USENIX, 1999, pp. 173–186.

D. Catteddu and G. Hogben, eds., *Cloud Computing: Benefits, Risks and Recommendations for Information Security*, European Network and Information Security Agency, 2009.

C. Clark et al., "Live Migration of Virtual Machines," *Proc. 2nd Symp. Networked Systems Design and Implementation*, USENIX, May 2005, pp. 273–286.

Cloud Security Alliance, *Top Threats to Cloud Computing*, vol. 1, Mar. 2010; https://cloudsecurityalliance.org/topthreats/csathreats.v1.0.pdf.

P. Colp et al., "Breaking Up is Hard to Do: Security and Functionality in a Commodity Hypervisor," *Proc. 23rd ACM Symp. Operating Systems Principles* (SOSP 11), ACM, Oct. 2011, pp. 189–202.

Department of Defense, *Trusted Computer System Evaluation Criteria*, DoD 5200.28-STD, Dec. 1985.

J.S. Fraga and D. Powell, "A fault- and intrusion-tolerant file system," *Proc. 3rd IFIP Int'l Conf. Computer Security*, Aug. 1985, pp. 203–218.

C. Gentry, "Fully Homomorphic Encryption Using Ideal Lattices," *Proc. 41st ACM Ann. Symp. Theory Computing* (STOC 09), ACM, 2009, pp. 169–178.

D. Grawrock, *Dynamics of a Trusted Platform: A Building Block Approach*, Intel Press, 2009.

E. Grosse et al., "Cloud Computing Roundtable," *IEEE Security and Privacy*, Nov./Dec. 2010, pp. 17–23.

M. Hanley et al., "An Analysis of Technical Observations in Insider Theft of Intellectual Property Cases," tech. report CMU/SEI-2011-TN-006, Software Eng. Inst., Carnegie Mellon Univ., 2011.

Intel Trusted Execution Technology (Intel TXT): Software Development Guide, document number 315168-008, Intel, Mar. 2011; http://download.intel.com/technology/security/downloads/315168.pdf.

W. Jansen and T. Grance, *Guidelines on Security and Privacy in Public Cloud Computing*, special publication 800-144, Nat'l Inst. Standards and Technology, Dec. 2011.

S. Kamara and K. Lauter, "Cryptographic Cloud Storage," *Proc. 14th Int'l Conf. Financial Cryptography and Data Security*, 2010, pp. 136–149.

L. Lamport, R. Shostak, and M. Pease, "The Byzantine generals problem," *ACM Trans. Programming Languages and Systems*, vol. 4, no. 3, July 1982, pp. 382–401.

K. Lauter, Naehrig, and V. Vaikuntanathan, "Can Homomorphic Encryption be Practical?," *Proc. 3rd ACM Cloud Computing Security Workshop* (CCSW 11), ACM, Oct. 2011, pp. 113–124.

P. Mahajan et al., "Depot: Cloud Storage with Minimal Trust," *Proc. 9th USENIX Symp. Operating Systems Design and Implementation* (OSDI 10), USENIX, Oct. 2010, pp. 307–322.

J.M. McCune et al., "TrustVisor: Efficient TCB Reduction and Attestation," *Proc. IEEE Symp. Security and Privacy* (SSP 10), IEEE CS, 2010, pp. 143–158.

P. Mell and T. Grance, *The NIST Definition of Cloud Computing (Draft)*, special publication 800-145 (draft), Nat'l Inst. Standards and Technology, Jan. 2011.

D.G. Murray, G. Milos, and S. Hand, "Improving Xen Security through Disaggregation," *Proc. 4th ACM SIGPLAN/SIGOPS Int'l Conf. Virtual Execution Environments* (VEE 08), ACM, 2008, pp. 151–160.

R. Neisse, D. Holling, and A. Pretschner, "Implementing Trust in Cloud Infrastructures," *Proc. 11th IEEE/ACM Int'l Symp. Cluster, Cloud and Grid Computing* (CCGRID), IEEE CS, May 2011, pp. 524–533.

A. Nguyen et al., "Delusional Boot: Securing Cloud Hypervisors without Massive Re-engineering," *Proc. European Conf. Computer Systems* (EuroSys 12), Apr. 2012, pp. 141–154.

B. Parno, "Trust Extension for Commodity Computers," *Communications of the ACM*, vol. 55, no. 6, June 2012, pp. 76–85.

B. Parno, J.M. McCune, and A. Perrig, *Bootstrapping Trust in Modern Computers*, Springer, 2011.

R.A. Popa et al., "CryptDB: Protecting Confidentiality with Encrypted Query Processing," *Proc. 23rd ACM Symp. Operating Systems Principles* (SOSP 2011), ACM, Oct. 2011, pp. 85–100.

T. Ristenpart et al., "Hey, You, Get Off of My Cloud: Exploring Information Leakage in Third-Party Compute Clouds," *Proc. 16th ACM Conf. Computer and Communications Security*, ACM, 2009, pp. 199–212.

F. Rocha and M. Correia, "Lucy in the Sky without Diamonds: Stealing Confidential Data in the Cloud," *Proc. 1st Int'l Workshop Dependability of Clouds, Data Centers and Virtual Computing Environments*, IEEE CS, June 2011, pp. 129–134.

M. Rosenblum and T. Garfinkel, "Virtual Machine Monitors: Current Technology and Future Trends," *Computer*, vol. 38, no. 5, May 2005, pp. 39–47.

N. Santos et al., "Policy-Sealed Data: A New Abstraction for Building Trusted Cloud Services," *Proc. 21st USENIX Security Symp.*, USENIX, Aug. 2012, p. 10.

N. Santos, K.P. Gummadi, and R. Rodrigues, "Towards Trusted Cloud Computing," *Proc. 1st Workshop Hot Topics in Cloud Computing* (HotCloud 09), USENIX, 2009; http://static.usenix.org/event/hotcloud09/tech/full_papers/santos.pdf.

U. Steinberg and B. Kauer, "NOVA: A Microhypervisor-Based Secure Virtualization Architecture," *Proc. 5th European Conf. Computer Systems* (EuroSys 10), ACM, 2010, pp. 209–222.

G. Strongin, "Trusted Computing Using AMD 'Pacifica' and 'Presidio' Secure Virtual Machine Technology," *Information Security Technical Report*, vol. 10, no. 2, Jan. 2005, pp. 120–132.

J. Szefer et al., "Eliminating the Hypervisor Attack Surface for a More Secure Cloud," *Proc. 18th ACM Conf. Computer and Communications Security* (CCS 2011), ACM, Oct. 2011, pp. 401–412.

Trusted Computing Group, *TPM Main Specification*, version 1.2, revision 103, 2007; www.trustedcomputinggroup.org/resources/tpm_main_specification.

M. van Dijk and A. Juels, "On the Impossibility of Cryptography Alone for Privacy-Preserving Cloud Computing," *Proc. 5th USENIX Conf. Hot Topics in Security*, USENIX, 2010, pp. 1–8.

P. Verissimo et al., "Intrusion-Resilient Middleware Design and Validation," *Information Assurance, Security and Privacy Services*, H. Raghav Rao and Shambhu Upadhyaya, eds., Emerald, 2009, pp. 615–678.

D. Wallom et al., "myTrustedCloud: Trusted Cloud Infrastructure for Security-critical Computation and Data Management," *Proc. 3rd IEEE Int'l. Conf. Cloud Computing Technology and Science* (CloudCom 11), IEEE CS, 2011, pp. 247–254.

Z. Wang and X. Jiang, "HyperSafe: A lightweight approach to provide lifetime hypervisor control-flow integrity," *Proc. IEEE Symp. Security and Privacy,* IEEE CS, May 2010, pp. 380–395.

F. Zhang et al., "CloudVisor: Retrofitting Protection of Virtual Machines in Multi-tenant Cloud with Nested Virtualization," *Proc. 23rd ACM Symp. Operating Systems Principles* (SOSP 11), ACM, Oct. 2011, pp. 203–216.

Acknowledgments

This work was partially supported by the Fundação para a Ciência e Tecnologia through the RC-Clouds (PCT/EIA-EIA/115211/2009) and PEst-OE/EEI/LA0021/2011 (INESC-ID) projects. We thank the partners of the EC TCLOUDS project and members of the Navigators group for many inspiring discussions on topics covered in this book. A preliminary version of this work appeared in *Computer*, vol. 44, no. 9, Sep. 2011, pp. 44–50.

About the Authors

Francisco Rocha is a second-year PhD student with the School of Computing Science at Newcastle University, UK. His research interests include systems security, software security, and security architectures. His latest work focuses on developing prevention techniques that guarantee memory confidentiality and integrity for cloud consumers in the presence of malicious insiders in cloud computing. Francisco holds an MSc in Information Technology – Information Security (MSIT-IS) from the Information Networking Institute at Carnegie Mellon University. Contact him at rocha.francisco@gmail.com.

Salvador Abreu is associate professor in the Department of Computer Science at the University of Évora and member of CENTRIA, the AI research center of the New University of Lisbon and University of Évora. He has participated in or coordinated research projects on logic and constraint programming, parallelism, and applications of declarative paradigms, including OAR, AJACS, HORUS, and CONTEMP. His research interests include declarative programming language design and application to hard combinatorial search problems, including intrusion detection as well as parallel and distributed computing models. Contact him at salvador. abreu@acm.org or via www.di.uevora.pt/~spa.

Miguel Correia is associate professor in the Instituto Superior Técnico at the Technical University of Lisbon and researcher in the Distributed Systems Group at INESC-ID. He has a PhD from Faculdade de Ciências, University of Lisbon. He has been involved in several international and national research projects related to cloud computing, intrusion tolerance, and security, including the TCLOUDS, MAF-TIA, and CRUTIAL projects, and in the ReSIST network of excellence. He has more than 100 publications, and his research interests include security, intrusion tolerance, distributed systems, cloud computing, and critical infrastructure protection. Contact him at miguel.p.correia@ist.utl.pt or via http://homepages. gsd.inesc-id.pt/~mpc.